The

Black Girl

Book

A book of Wisdom, Affirmations, Soul Medicine, and the Glow Up!

The Black Girl Book

Black Girl's Book of Wisdom: Lessons Life Has Taught Us & How We Grow from Them

When a Black Girl Wears Her Crown: Affirmations That Only a Black Girl Will Understand

Soul Medicine for a Black Girl: Conversations Between God & a Black Girl

When a Black Girl Glows Up: A 30-Day Conversation With Yourself

All rights reserved © 2019 by Ty Young

Presented by CIRCAPURPLE.COM in partnership with Young Dreams Publications

Proceeds go towards the Purple's Film Project campaign.

No part of this book may be reproduced or transmitted in any form or by any means, graphic, electronic, or mechanical, including photocopying, recording, taping, or by any information storage retrieval system, without the written permission of the publisher.

Author: Ty Young

Publisher: Young Dreams Publications, Chicago, IL
www.youngdreamsbig.com

ISBN: 978-0-578-49544-6
LCCN: TBD

Proceeds of this book go toward Purple's Film Project!

Campaign fundraiser for the documentary short film, *Saturday Flowers,* produced and directed by Ty Young!

To learn more and donate outside of this contribution please go to:
www.circapurple.com/purplesfilmproject

This book is dedicated to

The Black Girls!

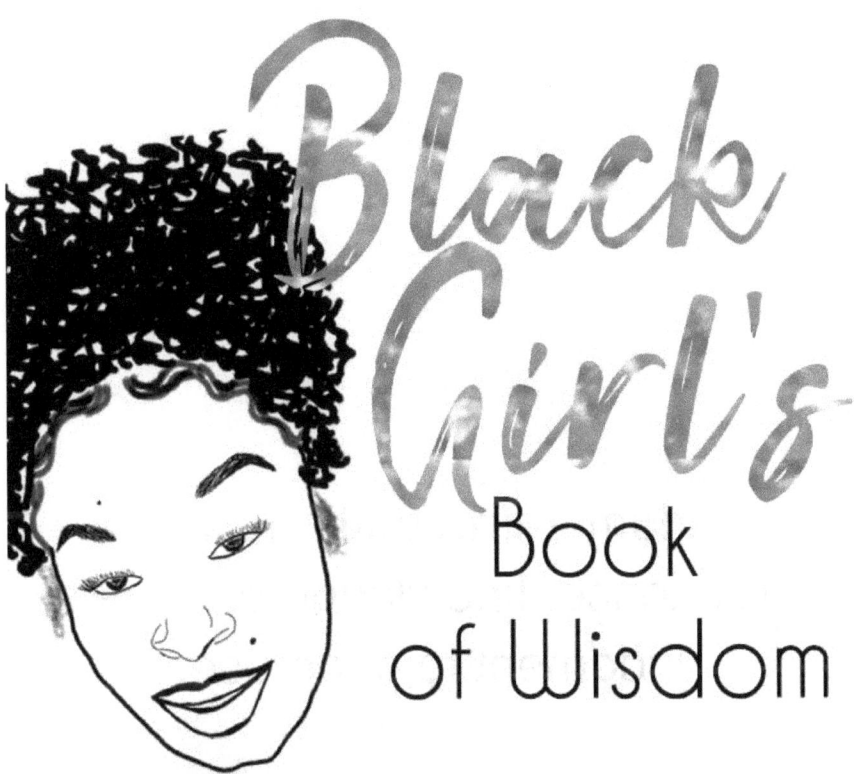

-circapurple presents-

Black Girl's Book of Wisdom

Lessons Life Has Taught Us & How We Grow From Them

purchase of this book supports purple's flower film project

Wisdom – (n.) putting all your experience, knowledge and good judgment to good use.

BLACK GIRL'S BOOK OF WISDOM

People often want to know how do you obtain wisdom? In my opinion, wisdom is not something you obtain specifically, but mostly a magical essence that embeds itself to those who choose to pay attention to life around them.

After you've gone through anything in life, good or bad, there's always a lesson in it. Wisdom is keeping what you've learned from those lessons tucked away to be used in the future.

When people ask us for our advice or opinion on something, what they're really asking us for is our wisdom.

Look at the book of Proverbs in the Bible. Though the Bible says that God gave Solomon a great abundance of wisdom, when you really look at how he applied his wisdom it was expressed based upon what he witnessed throughout his life.

The Bible proclaims that the "fear of the Lord is the beginning of wisdom" (Psalm 111:10). I truly understand why this is said. God is full of wisdom and the fear (or respect of his leadership and authority) means that you're submitting to being led in ultimate wisdom that will make you prosperous and successful throughout your life.

The reason I wrote this book of wisdom is because over the years I've learn a thing or two about people – especially in the areas of love and relationships. I used to be a woman that thrived on the functioning of my relationships and family dynamics.

I went through a season in my life where God stripped me of closeness with people. I was forced to get to know myself. Then once I learned a good chunk about who I was, it started to force me to observe man-kind.

CIRCAPURPLE PRESENTS

BLACK GIRL'S BOOK OF WISDOM

God forced me to do three things: see a situation, determined what I knew for sure about that person's character and situation, and what my real reality was beyond my feelings. Once I was able to successfully practice these three things with my eyes closed, I began to see things differently.

In the Black Girl series of books, this is just me sitting in who I am as a Black Girl and speaking my thoughts and feelings. I believe I have a lot to share, and I also believe that there are people who actually want to hear and read it.

As you read this book of wisdom don't just read it on a surface level, but really try to attune yourself into what is really being said. I have learned that wisdom is about looking beyond the surface and searching for the deeper. Sometimes the deeper is sitting in plain sight – but it's often overlooked because no one ever appreciates the obvious.

CIRCAPURPLE PRESENTS

BLACK GIRL'S BOOK OF WISDOM

When I learned to listen to my own voice, that's when
I truly discovered who I was.

CIRCAPURPLE PRESENTS

BLACK GIRL'S BOOK OF WISDOM

Unknowingly, we fight against the things that come to change us, not knowing we are prolonging our blessings from coming down from heaven.

CIRCAPURPLE PRESENTS

BLACK GIRL'S BOOK OF WISDOM

This is what I know about change. The universe sends signals to us expressing the need for change. Subconsciously, and often times consciously, we acknowledge this change. Once the universe is aware that we are aware that change needs to take place, it starts its mission to bring change to fruition.

As we continue to fight against change, we start this cycle of unfruitfulness. We often try to see how we can keep our old lives, the way we've always done things in our lives while also trying to bring the change into our lives, too. You simply can't do it. It's like putting on brand new clothes but you haven't washed up in 3 months. You're just a beautiful, smelly mess.

You must surrender! That's the only way to do it.

CIRCAPURPLE PRESENTS

BLACK GIRL'S BOOK OF WISDOM

You'll never know who you'll be until you try to become her.

Many of us are simply standing still, while a greater purpose is calling our names.

CIRCAPURPLE PRESENTS

BLACK GIRL'S BOOK OF WISDOM

Some people don't like that you're marching to the beat of your own drummer. The reason is because they're jealous because they don't have the courage to do it themselves.

Don't dismiss them, but if you have the energy help them find their courage.

CIRCAPURPLE PRESENTS

BLACK GIRL'S BOOK OF WISDOM

You must be OK with your cup overflowing.

CIRCAPURPLE PRESENTS

BLACK GIRL'S BOOK OF WISDOM

Ever try to fit a square into a circular opening? No matter how hard you try it just won't fit.

CIRCAPURPLE PRESENTS

BLACK GIRL'S BOOK OF WISDOM

You don't know what you don't know until you realize you don't know it.

I understood this after reading the book, *The Color Purple*.

CIRCAPURPLE PRESENTS

BLACK GIRL'S BOOK OF WISDOM

Allow yourself to cry about your disappointments. It's OK.

We all get disappointed. Shed the energy of the disappointment through the tears and be refreshed.

CIRCAPURPLE PRESENTS

BLACK GIRL'S BOOK OF WISDOM

No one owes you nothing. Everything you do should be done from the heart. Train your heart to be selfless.

We often times get heartbroken because we believe people owe us something because of what we do for them.

If you always want something for something, then you'll always be disappointed in man-kind. Your life will be lived in a much freer state when you change you – because changing people is nearly impossible and often takes an act of God.

CIRCAPURPLE PRESENTS

BLACK GIRL'S BOOK OF WISDOM

No one will think you're a punk for apologizing. They will feel relieved.

And those that feel like they've punked you because you apologized are emotionally immature and ultimately not worth your energy and maturity.

CIRCAPURPLE PRESENTS

BLACK GIRL'S BOOK OF WISDOM

EVERYONE has insecurities. Some are just better at hiding theirs.

Don't envy them because of their ability to hide. Be proud of yourself for the ability to be vulnerable.

However, there is a fine line between vulnerability and whining and seeking attention.

CIRCAPURPLE PRESENTS

BLACK GIRL'S BOOK OF WISDOM

Learn to love in a way that is beyond your heart. Your heart is where your emotions sit. Emotions don't always give the best advice.

A long-term, healthy relationship with your man is beyond what you feel in your heart. It's about understanding the person you are and the person you're with.

And the greatest characteristic you can have is patience.

CIRCAPURPLE PRESENTS

BLACK GIRL'S BOOK OF WISDOM

Struggle love is worth it, despite what many believe.

There's a difference between a toxic relationship and having difficulties in a relationship that both parties have to work through.

No relationship is 100% smooth sailing. There will always be a cycle of ups and downs. No one's life is always up, so if you couple yourself with someone you'll end up experiencing their downs, as well as their ups.

Take calculated risks in the area of love. Take sex off the table if you have the will power. Look at the man with eyes wide open and determine if the good outweighs the bad.

CIRCAPURPLE PRESENTS

BLACK GIRL'S BOOK OF WISDOM

When you allow anger and frustration to overwhelm you this is when you make some of the worst decisions of your life.

Learn how to center yourself so that you can make clear-minded decisions. Wise people have learned how to develop their patience to a level that they are not easily provoked by the uncertainty and constant changing of life.

BLACK GIRL'S BOOK OF WISDOM

Stop posting those subliminal memes and messages to him. He sees them but he doesn't care.

Period.

CIRCAPURPLE PRESENTS

Want to reach a man? Break your paragraphs up into largely spaced short sentences.

Not that he's an intelligent creature, but because men compartmentalize most things.

The fire you see in the relationship is often not his fire. He takes in little by little until he is capable of recognizing the real issue.

Again, this is were patience comes in. Yeah, yeah. I know the Facebook philosophers tell us that we shouldn't mother men and all that other stuff.

But men have been their way for centuries. Have they changed their thought process? No. And it's not going to change now because we've decided to stop mothering them or whatever it is claimed we're doing.

Evolution doesn't happen overnight. You know how many decades we'd have to endure before men evolve into what we attempt to change them into?

BLACK GIRL'S BOOK OF WISDOM

That feeling you feel is the desire to want to be chosen. It's a natural feeling. Embrace it and acknowledge it.

But also tell the heart that you may not get chosen and prepare to move on and start over.

Straight, no chaser.

BLACK GIRL'S BOOK OF WISDOM

Don't waste your time trying to impress people. Those that need be impressed aren't genuinely interested in your cause. They just need to feel important.

Rather focus on those who authentically gravitate toward you in sincerity.

People are afraid to be vulnerable with us because we have proven ourselves to not handle their vulnerability with care. People have to be able to trust that we won't take their deepest, darkest, open part of them and mishandle it.

If you wonder why people don't open up to you, revisit the last interaction with someone that was vulnerable with you.

BLACK GIRL'S BOOK OF WISDOM

In the heat of an argument, never ever throw someone's shortcomings or insecurities in their face.

It makes them stay on guard every time they speak to you because they want to be ready to protect their pride.

CIRCAPURPLE PRESENTS

BLACK GIRL'S BOOK OF WISDOM

Get a life. Don't be all up under that man all the time.

For some, the reason you get upset every time he leaves is because deep down you don't trust him. Your subconscious believes that as long as he's with you, in your presence, he's not cheating.

That's not the best way to be in a relationship.

CIRCAPURPLE PRESENTS

BLACK GIRL'S BOOK OF WISDOM

Talking, listening, and comprehending are the keys that brings quality into a relationship.

When they talk you get to listen to what they're heart feels. When you comprehend you can understand their why.

Learning to have empathy affords you the ability to have patience with people. We've been taught to not have patience with people because it is believed they should know better.

However, some people weren't raised right – and that's not their fault.

CIRCAPURPLE PRESENTS

BLACK GIRL'S BOOK OF WISDOM

It's OK if you choose to hang in there with someone through their tough times. Just make sure that you are emotionally strong to endure it. Don't build someone else up at the expense of your own happiness.

Be brave enough to admit that you're unable to help them.

CIRCAPURPLE PRESENTS

BLACK GIRL'S BOOK OF WISDOM

Our children are constantly expressing their pain. Their emotional immaturity causes them to not articulate it in the best way. Sometimes you must humble yourself in order to hear them clearly.

CIRCAPURPLE PRESENTS

BLACK GIRL'S BOOK OF WISDOM

Cry, girl! It cleanses your soul. You are not weak for crying. Jesus cried in the garden because he was real about what he was feeling.

He had enough sense to tell God he didn't want to do it. Being honest gave him strength.

CIRCAPURPLE PRESENTS

BLACK GIRL'S BOOK OF WISDOM

Sometimes you have to help him communicate. It's OK.

We'll often give strangers more help than the people who are closest to us. That's a shame.

CIRCAPURPLE PRESENTS

BLACK GIRL'S BOOK OF WISDOM

Trust me. You have more power over negative people by ignoring them than engaging with the same energy.

Their ego is wrap around the ability to knock people off their square. Help bring them down a peg.

CIRCAPURPLE PRESENTS

BLACK GIRL'S BOOK OF WISDOM

Trust me, everyone is hypocritical at some point in their lives. Someone can attempt to make you feel bad for wearing shorts, while they're standing in a two-piece bikini.

This judgment from them is not always intentional. Some people have foggy mirrors. It's not your job to help them clear the fog. But it is your job to know your own voice and stand on what you hear from yourself.

You'll lose yourself and be walking around unhappy listening to people who have foggy mirrors.

CIRCAPURPLE PRESENTS

The need for closure is sometimes about the ego.

And sometimes we want people to apologize to us for things we did to ourselves. Example: We stayed in a relationship too long that should have ended ages ago. We get mad at the person for leaving because we've made up in our mind that they owed us a miserable commitment.

The reality is you're mad at yourself because you didn't leave first.

When a Black Girl Wears Her Crown

-circapurple presents-

Affirmations That Only A Black Girl Will Understand

purchase of this book supports purple's flower film project

Affirmation – (n.) the action or process of affirming something or being affirmed; emotional support or encouragement

WHEN A BLACK GIRL WEARS HER CROWN

The law of attractions says that whatever we think, believe, and feel will come to us. When declaring our daily affirmations, we must believe that we are worthy of the words we affirm to ourselves.

In a world where the Black Girl is constantly fighting for a place, I decided that I was going to affirm my own place, values, and acceptance.

This may be funny to some, but I've found this place of affirmations from two polar opposite places – The Word of God and Solange.

The Bible has been saying to us for a very long time to speak positively to ourselves, but it appears I've been missing this message.

Well, I haven't been missing the message entirely, but as of recently it has really penetrated my heart that I must speak life into my life.

Let me give you a few examples of what I mean...

> Proverbs 18:21 Death and life are in the power of the tongue...
>
> Proverbs 23:7 For as he thinketh in his heart, so is he...
>
> 2 Corinthians 12:10 ...for when I am weak, then am I strong.
>
> Ephesians 5:19 Speaking to yourselves in psalms and hymns and spiritual songs, singing and making melody in your heart to the Lord...

After thinking about those scriptures, I realized that the Bible has been teaching us about the law of attraction, but I have

WHEN A BLACK GIRL WEARS HER CROWN

been missing it. Clearly, God meant what he said and he wants to reiterate to us that whatever we think that is what will come to us.

God said, "WATCH YOUR MOUTH!"

Now let me explain the Solange phenomenon. I hate to even have to break it down like this, but if you don't know who Solange is let me tell you. She is aka Solange Knowles, aka, Sol-Angel, aka Solo, aka Beyoncé's Little Sister (my least favorite name).

OK, now that that's out of the way…

I have followed Solange's career for a very long time. My bias disclaimer: We share the same birthday, June 24. Even before I realized we had the same birthday it was something about her that I was drawn to.

She has this effortless ability to follow the beat of her own drummer. While some view her as strange, eccentric, or too out the box, these very characteristics she possesses have seemed to cause her to live her best life.

She appears to be her most happiest and freest self because she affirms her life in the realm that she requires, and not what others thinks she should. It's often said that the most happiest people are those that don't care what other people think.

I appreciate a person who is comfortable in their own skin and can proudly wear it in the beauty that God meant for it to be lived in.

You may wonder how does this relate to affirmations and the law of attraction? In my mind here's how I bridge the two.

WHEN A BLACK GIRL WEARS HER CROWN

Your affirmations are the thoughts, imaginations, and aspirations that you need that will allow you to be your most happiest and freest self.
What do you believe you deserve?

What is God's plan for your life?

What should your reality look like?

Only you can answer these questions. But being the inspirational being that I am, I'm going to give you some positive affirmations to help you unlock the answers to these questions. As you delve into these affirmations it is my prayer that it helps you to look within yourself to really pull out of your inner-being the answers to those three life changing questions.

Seriously, once you begin to answer the questions for yourself and begin to put actions to those questions – YOUR LIFE WILL CHANGE!

When A Black Girl Wears Her Crown means to be exactly who think you're supposed to be.

Now, I will be honest, in the beginning some of us will have to fake it until we make it. And that's just an honest approach to this. Many of us have been walking in defeat for a very long time so we have to reprogram our minds to think differently.

Every single word you speak has a destination. Every single thought has a purpose. The Bible tells us all the time to cast down evil imagination. Unfortunately, God can't reach into your brain and take that away from you – this is something you have to do.

Speaking life is just that – speaking life. Don't say what you don't want. Say what you want. Don't think about what you don't want. Think about what you want.

CIRCAPURPLE PRESENTS

WHEN A BLACK GIRL WEARS HER CROWN

Ex. Don't say, "I don't want to be in debt anymore." Say, "I have enough money to meet all my needs and more."

For a little while some of our lives' present realities will contradict the words we speak and thoughts we have, but we must take our example from God. He spoke those things that were not as if they were, his words obeyed him and did not come back void. God is in you and he wants you to be as his is – speaking life and not death.

Wearing your crown only comes effortless after you've diligently practiced walking with it on and purposefully put it only every day.

So, are you ready?

Let's get into it!

CIRCAPURPLE PRESENTS

WHEN A BLACK GIRL WEARS HER CROWN

Spiritual Being

In the Bible, God used different women for different purposes. They all had a spiritual purpose in the Kingdom.

There is a spiritual energy residing in you that must find its way into this world so that you can bless nations.

Back in the day, *Big Mamas* were so special because they understood how to tap into this energy and allowed it to flow.

CIRCAPURPLE PRESENTS

WHEN A BLACK GIRL WEARS HER CROWN

I am the balm, black castor oil, 'tussin', 7-Up, Vicks, Epsom salt, Vaseline, apple cider vinegar, honey and lemon, aloe vera that can heal right down to the very soul of everyone that I come into contact with. My energy is so healing, that all my loved ones have to do is lay in my bosom and receive the phenomenon that is me.

CIRCAPURPLE PRESENTS

WHEN A BLACK GIRL WEARS HER CROWN

I am the being that God himself made to speak prayers that reaches heaven.

CIRCAPURPLE PRESENTS

WHEN A BLACK GIRL WEARS HER CROWN

I am one with my Creator. The illuminating glow makes my black girl magic brighter.

CIRCAPURPLE PRESENTS

WHEN A BLACK GIRL WEARS HER CROWN

I vibrate to the highest frequency because my soul is cleansed.

CIRCAPURPLE PRESENTS

WHEN A BLACK GIRL WEARS HER CROWN

I am renewed daily, and virtue is replaced because I relinquish my entire being to God and allow him to build me up to my highest potential.

CIRCAPURPLE PRESENTS

WHEN A BLACK GIRL WEARS HER CROWN

I am a temple that houses the magnificence, glory, power, and righteousness that is God. I have a nurturing energy that feeds the soul of those around me and protects my heart, mind, spirit, and soul.

CIRCAPURPLE PRESENTS

WHEN A BLACK GIRL WEARS HER CROWN

I am absolutely, unequivocally everything that God designed me to be.

CIRCAPURPLE PRESENTS

WHEN A BLACK GIRL WEARS HER CROWN

Health

Health in the Black community is a battle that we continue to fight. Rather it is obesity, diet, ailments, or any other disease that plagues us, we are constantly fighting. I have to admit, on many occasions I have looked in the mirror and said to myself, "Ewww, I'm fat." Clearly, I'm not wearing my crown.

We have struggled with body image issues as well because we've allowed the standard of beauty definition to define us. We reject ourselves as if we're not beautiful just the way God made us. We've told ourselves so many lies that some of us don't know who we are when it comes to health.

But today that stops now!

CIRCAPURPLE PRESENTS

WHEN A BLACK GIRL WEARS HER CROWN

I exercise and eat healthy because my black girl magic deserves a perfected vessel – and I look divine naked.

CIRCAPURPLE PRESENTS

WHEN A BLACK GIRL WEARS HER CROWN

I love myself more than the desire to neglect myself.

CIRCAPURPLE PRESENTS

WHEN A BLACK GIRL WEARS HER CROWN

There's no way my version of beauty is flawed because God don't make no mistakes! I am the standard!

CIRCAPURPLE PRESENTS

WHEN A BLACK GIRL WEARS HER CROWN

I am the healthiest version of me because I cook my collard greens and cornbread and other soul food the right way.

CIRCAPURPLE PRESENTS

WHEN A BLACK GIRL WEARS HER CROWN

I have the energy and stamina I need to meet all of my exercise and mental obligations.

CIRCAPURPLE PRESENTS

WHEN A BLACK GIRL WEARS HER CROWN

Since I've been taking care of my body, my edges are growing back, my skin is glowing, my nails are beautiful, and my waist is snatched!

WHEN A BLACK GIRL WEARS HER CROWN

I won the battle over depression and mental fog because I detoxed my body and put nutrients in. I moved around negative energy and people. Good. Vibes. Only.

CIRCAPURPLE PRESENTS

WHEN A BLACK GIRL WEARS HER CROWN

Family

Our families are important to us. Some of us have been battling generational curses and pathologies that hinder our future generations.

But the cycles stop now with you. As you affirm yourself and family into a better future, the generations to come will benefit from it.

CIRCAPURPLE PRESENTS

WHEN A BLACK GIRL WEARS HER CROWN

My family understands what communication is.

CIRCAPURPLE PRESENTS

WHEN A BLACK GIRL WEARS HER CROWN

My sons and daughters understand healthy family dynamics and know how to have compassion toward one another.

CIRCAPURPLE PRESENTS

WHEN A BLACK GIRL WEARS HER CROWN

My entire family has A1 credit.

CIRCAPURPLE PRESENTS

WHEN A BLACK GIRL WEARS HER CROWN

My family thrives abundantly!

CIRCAPURPLE PRESENTS

WHEN A BLACK GIRL WEARS HER CROWN

I am overjoyed that my family knows our fathers and they're visible, reachable, and pour into us.

CIRCAPURPLE PRESENTS

WHEN A BLACK GIRL WEARS HER CROWN

I have faith in my family, just like I have faith in my religion.

CIRCAPURPLE PRESENTS

WHEN A BLACK GIRL WEARS HER CROWN

I am celebrating that my family has a legacy of business, wealth, and success!

CIRCAPURPLE PRESENTS

WHEN A BLACK GIRL WEARS HER CROWN

Finance

Can we break out of the stigma of having bad credit and not knowing how to handle our finances? It's depressing. We have to learn how to deal with money in order to have a fair chance in this world.

We're changing the game right now!

CIRCAPURPLE PRESENTS

WHEN A BLACK GIRL WEARS HER CROWN

I am the bomb at saving money!

CIRCAPURPLE PRESENTS

WHEN A BLACK GIRL WEARS HER CROWN

I get excited knowing my bank account doubles itself every month! And there's always enough to go 'round!

CIRCAPURPLE PRESENTS

WHEN A BLACK GIRL WEARS HER CROWN

My bank account looks like Oprah's – period!

CIRCAPURPLE PRESENTS

WHEN A BLACK GIRL WEARS HER CROWN

I always practice mature spending habits, and fabulously live within my means.

CIRCAPURPLE PRESENTS

WHEN A BLACK GIRL WEARS HER CROWN

I naturally attract abundance and my cup continues to overflow.

CIRCAPURPLE PRESENTS

WHEN A BLACK GIRL WEARS HER CROWN

I am the bank! And I give wisely and gracefully!

CIRCAPURPLE PRESENTS

WHEN A BLACK GIRL WEARS HER CROWN

I am relaxed knowing that I want for nothing – and even in want My Father supplies all!

CIRCAPURPLE PRESENTS

WHEN A BLACK GIRL WEARS HER CROWN

Career

Look here, it's no secret that Black Girls are not only multifaceted, but we're multi-talented. We can be absolutely anything in this world that we want.

Some of us lack the fortitude needed to push through. These affirmations are designed to help all my Black Girls push and excel.

CIRCAPURPLE PRESENTS

WHEN A BLACK GIRL WEARS HER CROWN

I am the Black Girl in charge!

CIRCAPURPLE PRESENTS

WHEN A BLACK GIRL WEARS HER CROWN

I don't need anyone's validation but my own!

CIRCAPURPLE PRESENTS

WHEN A BLACK GIRL WEARS HER CROWN

I surround myself around genuine, authentic people who drive me to be successful!

CIRCAPURPLE PRESENTS

WHEN A BLACK GIRL WEARS HER CROWN

I understand fully what I want to do with my career – and it will not be patterned after anyone else's!

CIRCAPURPLE PRESENTS

WHEN A BLACK GIRL WEARS HER CROWN

I love knowing that I am in control of my life. Just because momma, auntie, and 'nem did it like this or that, I have permission to do it in my own way.

CIRCAPURPLE PRESENTS

WHEN A BLACK GIRL WEARS HER CROWN

My influence is like Beyoncé's! I will not lose!

CIRCAPURPLE PRESENTS

WHEN A BLACK GIRL WEARS HER CROWN

I don't have to ride the coattail of the next best thing or upcoming *it girl* – I am the next best thing! Therefore, I ride my own coattail!

CIRCAPURPLE PRESENTS

WHEN A BLACK GIRL WEARS HER CROWN

Relationships

In today's society we are so quick to cancel someone! Due to our upbringing, we have not learned proper communication skills or conflict resolution skills

But today we're learning to be virtuous Black Girls! We may not be able to win over every relationship, but we will not be the one who is responsible for its downfall!

CIRCAPURPLE PRESENTS

WHEN A BLACK GIRL WEARS HER CROWN

I am comfortable with vulnerability because I recognize it is my super power!

CIRCAPURPLE PRESENTS

WHEN A BLACK GIRL WEARS HER CROWN

I will not let life, nor the demands of others rush me!

CIRCAPURPLE PRESENTS

WHEN A BLACK GIRL WEARS HER CROWN

My grace is like Michelle Obama's and that's what attracts prosperous relationships toward me!

CIRCAPURPLE PRESENTS

WHEN A BLACK GIRL WEARS HER CROWN

I am so blessed to have cherished and harmonious relationships with my friends!

CIRCAPURPLE PRESENTS

WHEN A BLACK GIRL WEARS HER CROWN

I am positive that my friends love me because they know I am the vault to all their secrets, and they receive a special love from me!

CIRCAPURPLE PRESENTS

WHEN A BLACK GIRL WEARS HER CROWN

I love that my circle is so tight that no one can penetrate us! I am my Black Girls' keeper!

CIRCAPURPLE PRESENTS

WHEN A BLACK GIRL WEARS HER CROWN

I aspired that, even in times of disagreements, my friends and I don't let anything destroy our wonderful and blessed relationships!

CIRCAPURPLE PRESENTS

WHEN A BLACK GIRL WEARS HER CROWN

Love

Rather you're single and waiting or in love with your man we must always be in tuned with who we are so that we're a positive force in the area of love.

I like to say that love is a luxury that we all can afford. But what you do with that luxury totally depends on the state of your emotional maturity.

CIRCAPURPLE PRESENTS

WHEN A BLACK GIRL WEARS HER CROWN

Contentment is my crown and love are my jewels!

CIRCAPURPLE PRESENTS

WHEN A BLACK GIRL WEARS HER CROWN

I am emotionally stable.

CIRCAPURPLE PRESENTS

WHEN A BLACK GIRL WEARS HER CROWN

Love and life are my portions! God said I deserved it!

CIRCAPURPLE PRESENTS

WHEN A BLACK GIRL WEARS HER CROWN

I'm the best thing that ever happened to anyone!

CIRCAPURPLE PRESENTS

WHEN A BLACK GIRL WEARS HER CROWN

I'm so happy because my man understands me! Our relationship is tranquil because of this understanding.

CIRCAPURPLE PRESENTS

WHEN A BLACK GIRL WEARS HER CROWN

All my petals says that he loves me!

CIRCAPURPLE PRESENTS

WHEN A BLACK GIRL WEARS HER CROWN

Me and my man's love is more than just a feeling in the heart! It's an invisible essence that is created on a mental level. We can live without each other while yet still choose one another.

CIRCAPURPLE PRESENTS

Soul Medicine – (n.) a spiritual antidote for the healing of the inner soul.

SOUL MEDICINE FOR A BLACK GIRL

Ever had some hard questions that you were afraid to ask God? I know I have. We're taught that we must always reverence and fear God. This belief has caused us to believe that it's unacceptable to question God.

While I'm very caution about how I present some of my concerns and lack of understanding about things to God, I've learned that God wants us to come to him.

He said in his word that we should never lean to our own understanding (Proverbs 3:5-6, KJV), and if we lack wisdom about a thing to ask him about it (James 1:5, KJV). So why again are you afraid to ask God the hard questions?

The reason why I came up with *Soul Medicine for a Black Girl* is because I recognize the power in talking to God. When I don't understand things I just flat out talk to God.

When we think of medicine, we think of something that is prescribed to us by a doctor that we ingest. However, often these medications aren't cures, but merely remedies that manage symptoms. Through conversations with God, I've found that he is able to cure my soul. And I'm not just talking in the biblical/spiritual sense of heaven and hell, but in the sense of rooting up the things that makes my soul sick and causes me heartache and pain.

You can't get healed unless you open your mouth and tell the doctor you're sick. And sometimes telling the doctor you're sick is telling him about some uncomfortable, awkward symptoms.

Sometimes the symptoms can be so ugly that to some they may come off as disrespectful. But when you serve God like I know him, you won't allow this to stop you from speaking your truth.

SOUL MEDICINE FOR A BLACK GIRL

Sometimes I do prep what I'm about to say to God with this phrase, "God, I'm coming humbly to you and in no way am I trying to be insubordinate or disrespectful, but…"
As we have our conversation – which consist of me speaking out loud to him as if I'm talking to a physical person and him speaking softly inaudibly to my spirit – he helps me to understand things.

I don't always get an answer right away, though. Sometimes the answer to my concern or lack of wisdom comes through the demonstration of his power. Things will happen that could only be explain as the move of God in my life, and then he'll remind me of when we had *that talk* and I recognize he was answering my prayer.

Your closeness to God is totally dependent upon how honest and up-close and personal you want to get with him. You must intentionally anticipate for God to answer you. Because he has such a loud, silent presence, I'm always aware of the world around me – because through it is how he speaks.

I've learned to listen to everything and everybody because I know he'll use anything to declare a thing to me.

These are real conversation between a Black Girl and God.

What you're going to receive in this book is unfiltered prayers from a Black Girl who has questioned God and received his answer. In the later part of the book are questions that are designed for you to ask God for yourself and allow him to present to you his answer.

These are not a sugar-coated, religiously, politically correct conversations. These are conversations that most Christians wouldn't dare have as a conversation out loud with anyone.

SOUL MEDICINE FOR A BLACK GIRL

Dear God,

Sometimes, I think I think too much, or too large, or too abundantly, or too vividly.

Your Word tells me that you can do abundantly above all I can ask or think. I promise I don't mean to sound ungrateful of all the things you've done for me because there absolutely have been times that you've blown my mind.

But there are some things I've thought about and I'm still waiting for the abundant blessing. I've asked for things before and you sure enough blessed me, but it wasn't abundantly.

Again, I'm not trying to come off ungrateful. I'm sure this is the flesh talking because the spirit inside of me would never come at you like this. But I have real questions. At first, I didn't want to bother you about this, but I'm sure you were aware that I was thinking it anyway. So, I'm just going to keep it 100 with you.

I'm trying to examine myself to get an understanding of why I wasn't deserving of the abundant blessings. Did I do something wrong? Did my thoughts not line up with yours?

I'm just asking...

• •

Hey Daughter,

I hear you. No, you don't think too much, too large, too abundantly, or too vividly. You're doing what is natural to you.

But I ask you to trust me as your creator and trust that I know what's best for you. Regardless of how you believe or imagine that you should be blessed, understand that every time I bless you, regardless of the magnitude or smallness, that you're receiving my abundance. I'm a perfect God and my blessings

SOUL MEDICINE FOR A BLACK GIRL

are perfect and exactly what you need at any given specific time. And that reason alone makes it abundantly above all you can ask or think.

Love ya.

SOUL MEDICINE FOR A BLACK GIRL

God, the older saints have proclaimed about your miracles – being a doctor in the sick room, a lawyer in the court room – but I've yet to see that in my own life.

Have you withdrawn this power that so heavily rested on the saints in the later time or am I missing it?

There have been so many situations that I've prayed about that I needed you to turn around for me, but I never saw your hand. Am I doing something wrong? Is my salvation tainted in some way that I forfeit your power in my life?

∎∎

My Love, you never pay attention.

Remember when you didn't have the money to pay your light bill and your lights should have gotten cut off, but for some reason when you called the light company for an extension and you miraculously had credit on your account?

I saw you ahead of time having financial issue in this season. So, I orchestrated an error on your part of double paying on your bill two year ago. One payment was posted properly and the other was *lost in the system*. I have a saint that works at the light company who was auditing, and I had her find your *lost payment* and properly post it to your account.

Stop saying you don't see the miracles in your life and learn to look deeper. You take a lot of things for granted and this is why you miss the smallest miracles I perform on your behalf.

SOUL MEDICINE FOR A BLACK GIRL

Lord, I'm having an anxiety attack.

I feel suffocated by the demands of me as a Black Girl and being in the Black Church. I love worship, the praise of your Holy Name, and the anointing of your Word. But I struggle with your people and legalistic principles.

I often feel like I'm amongst a bunch of Sadducees and Pharisees. Everyone knows the Word, but I don't find too many people living it. We're taught that we shouldn't look at people and what they do but have our own personal relationship with you. This has become very difficult for me to do because your people have hurt me. I'm sure I've hurt some people, too.

So many people have told me how I should be living my life in you, but then when the veil is ripped back, I find that their lives are full of hypocrisy. How do you explain that?

I want to explore other things outside of the tradition of church, but I feel so judged about it. What am to do?

••

My child, have you truly studied the life and walk of Jesus?

Have you truly digested the teaching of Paul in the New Testament?

I created you to be like no one but yourself.

Just as the Sadducees and Pharisees were stuck on tradition, new saints are no different. Learn to decipher what is holy commanded to you through me and what is express solely through the flesh of man.

Once you can separate the two, your experience in me will be much more enjoyable.

SOUL MEDICINE FOR A BLACK GIRL

God, my marriage didn't last, and I'm pissed about it.

I thought I did everything right. I fasted, I prayed, I tried to be a good godly wife to him. I was so willing to be there through death do us part – even though I, too, was miserable.

How come you didn't keep my marriage from falling apart? Why didn't you save it? You said the king's heart was in your hands, you couldn't turn this one around?

••

Daughter, what I am not is a puppet master.

I deal with the matters and condition of one's heart as it's susceptible and open to me.

Just because you were willing to stay in a marriage that was miserable, doesn't mean he was obligated to do the same. I have called everyone to peace.

Also, when I looked into his heart there was nothing there for you. I can't do anything about that. If there were something there, surely, I could have worked that thing out.

I know this is a harsh word, but that is the reality of it.

I understand that you are hurt, and my job as a father is to help you heal. However, I can't help you heal through something that you want to hold on to.

Just like I wouldn't make you stay with someone that was abusing you if you didn't want to stay, I'm must give him the same respect.

Go back and revisit the marriage. See what you did right and wrong, open your eyes and see the person you were married to. Take the lessons and learn from them for your next marriage.

SOUL MEDICINE FOR A BLACK GIRL

God, I just want to be happy.

■■■

You'll never experience true happiness until you give your all to me.

SOUL MEDICINE FOR A BLACK GIRL

What I've come to understand about God is that he's realistic and he takes the condition of a person's heart seriously.

Ever known someone that does some stupid things or make very irrational decisions, but when you really look at them you see that they really have a good heart? That's how God deals with us. Everything he does for us is pivoted on our hearts. Through this teaching I've learned to look at people through this lens and what I know about their hearts.

A lot of times our actions, not our words, determine what's in our hearts.

I've learned to talk to God about people's hearts. I've learned to ask him to reveal to me why people do certain things that they do. In this world, it's so easy to get jaded by the actions of people. We would lump people into these groups without breaking them down into the individuals that God intended them to be.

God has taught me how to use empathy. Just as I want to be understood, others want to be understood as well. Just as I have pathologies, others have them as well.

Having conversations with God is not just about pointing out all the negative things in your life, or life around you. But genuinely and purposefully attempting to get a better understanding about the life we're living.

I've had a fantasy about what life is supposed to be like, until I began to have realistic conversations with God.

As the Creator of life, who else would be the authority on the topic of human nature and ideologies? He sits high and looks low, and well-aware of the flawed individuals we are.

We put way too much trust in man, and this is way they disappoint us so much. My pastor would preach all the time that people shouldn't have our hearts. This is not to be confused with that we shouldn't love people and that we shouldn't develop deep connections with people – because we absolutely should. But through my conversations with God, I've learned and understood this notion clearer about not giving people my heart.

When I used to fall in love, I would feel this sickening feeling in my heart. It would be filled with so much passion, chaotic energy, and forceful desire. The love for that person would consume me and if anything went wrong in the relationship, I would feel like I was going to die.

One day in a conversation with God, he told me that was unhealthy. He asked me a simple question: "Should love hinder your ability to think straight?"

That was an eye-opening question. Because he was right, love shouldn't have had that much control over me that I lost my ability to make sound decisions.

In my conversation with God, he explained to me that I should look at all of his examples of love in the Bible and patterned my love after that. What I learned in patterning my love-style after God's was that you must couple it with having a magical ability to see and accept reality and have empathy.

I'm going to always reference back to the word empathy because it's a powerful tool when used correctly.

The five prayer examples are real conversations I've had with God, but next will be a challenge to have your own personal conversations with God. There are a lot of things that we can ask him but are afraid, but it's important that we ask him so that we can have spiritual clarity in our lives.

There is no particular order to ask these questions. Whatever season you are in you should ask the questions that resonate with you the most.

SOUL MEDICINE FOR A BLACK GIRL

Do know that God doesn't always answer right away. Sometimes answers come days, weeks, months, years later – but the point is to ask the question and give things over to God.

When I ask God questions, whatever other thought are provoked by the question I speak those too. You'll be amazed at the clarity God will give you just by having a simple conversation. Talk to him just like you would your girlfriend on the phone. I promise he'll speak back in his own little way.

SOUL MEDICINE FOR A BLACK GIRL

Prayer:

God, what is your will for my love life?

Deeply explore this question with God. This may cause for you to go on an extended consecration and/or fast before the Lord. Trust his process.

It is not my belief that we have to live loveless lives in the Lord. But sometimes our wait is much longer than some of our other sisters. We have to come to a place of acceptance and contentment with whatever God says.

What did you and God talk about? (write it here or in your journal)

_____

_____

_____

_____

_____

_____

_____

_____

_____

_____

_____

SOUL MEDICINE FOR A BLACK GIRL

SOUL MEDICINE FOR A BLACK GIRL

SOUL MEDICINE FOR A BLACK GIRL

Prayer:

God, am I a good friend to my friends?

Deeply explore this question with God. This may cause for you to go on an extended consecration and/or fast before the Lord. Trust his process.

Let's face it, some of us have toxic energy and ways. Some of it is not our fault, it's learned behavior that we must correct.

What did you and God talk about? (write it here or in your journal)

_____

_____

_____

_____

_____

_____

_____

_____

_____

_____

_____

_____

SOUL MEDICINE FOR A BLACK GIRL

SOUL MEDICINE FOR A BLACK GIRL

SOUL MEDICINE FOR A BLACK GIRL

Prayer:

God, why is my womb barren? And what am I supposed to do about it?

Deeply explore this question with God. This may cause for you to go on an extended consecration and/or fast before the Lord. Trust his process.

Fertility issues plague our Black Women. Many struggle with this, and often times privately. Only God knows why some have been burdened with this issue and he's the only one who can fix it.

What did you and God talk about? (write it here or in your journal)

_____

_____

_____

_____

_____

_____

_____

_____

_____

_____

SOUL MEDICINE FOR A BLACK GIRL

SOUL MEDICINE FOR A BLACK GIRL

SOUL MEDICINE FOR A BLACK GIRL

Prayer:

God, reveal the truth behind my church hurt?

Deeply explore this question with God. This may cause for you to go on an extended consecration and/or fast before the Lord. Trust his process.

Many of us have allowed our relationship with God to be tainted by church hurt. However, the root cause could be much deeper than *what someone did to us*. We must seek God to get to the root of our real hurt.

What did you and God talk about? (write it here or in your journal)

_____

_____

_____

_____

_____

_____

_____

_____

_____

_____

_____

SOUL MEDICINE FOR A BLACK GIRL

SOUL MEDICINE FOR A BLACK GIRL

SOUL MEDICINE FOR A BLACK GIRL

Prayer:

God, can I really only date saved men? There are no men in the church, why can't I have a morally decent boyfriend?

Deeply explore this question with God. This may cause for you to go on an extended consecration and/or fast before the Lord. Trust his process.

Women outnumber men in the Black church, which leaves many of us man-less. We come across good men outside of the church all the time, but the *church* says we shouldn't partake. This is a struggle for a lot of single Black Church Girls.

What did you and God talk about? (write it here or in your journal)

_____

_____

_____

_____

_____

_____

_____

_____

_____

SOUL MEDICINE FOR A BLACK GIRL

SOUL MEDICINE FOR A BLACK GIRL

SOUL MEDICINE FOR A BLACK GIRL

Prayer:

God, why do I love drama?

Deeply explore this question with God. This may cause for you to go on an extended consecration and/or fast before the Lord. Trust his process.

Again, back to being toxic. Some us want love, but because dysfunction is familiar to us, we always find ourselves involved in some drama. We truly don't mean to be toxic, but unfortunately it's part of the fabric of some of our DNA. Let's help God change us.

What did you and God talk about? (write it here or in your journal)

_____

_____

_____

_____

_____

_____

_____

_____

_____

_____

SOUL MEDICINE FOR A BLACK GIRL

SOUL MEDICINE FOR A BLACK GIRL

SOUL MEDICINE FOR A BLACK GIRL

Prayer:

God, when will I get my winning season?

Deeply explore this question with God. This may cause for you to go on an extended consecration and/or fast before the Lord. Trust his process.

We watch so many around us win, and we're doing the most just to stay in a positive state-of-mind while our personal lives are in shambles. Sometimes you just want a win, any win that will keep you encouraged.

What did you and God talk about? (write it here or in your journal)

_____

_____

_____

_____

_____

_____

_____

_____

_____

_____

SOUL MEDICINE FOR A BLACK GIRL

SOUL MEDICINE FOR A BLACK GIRL

SOUL MEDICINE FOR A BLACK GIRL

Prayer:

God, I struggle with traditional church. How do I deal with this?

Deeply explore this question with God. This may cause for you to go on an extended consecration and/or fast before the Lord. Trust his process.

For some Black Girls, stepping into the sanctuary is a hard task. The yearn for a connection and relationship with God is there, but digesting church in the traditional sense doesn't cut it for them.

What did you and God talk about? (write it here or in your journal)

_____

_____

_____

_____

_____

_____

_____

_____

_____

_____

SOUL MEDICINE FOR A BLACK GIRL

_____
_____
_____
_____
_____
_____
_____
_____
_____
_____
_____
_____
_____
_____
_____
_____
_____
_____
_____

SOUL MEDICINE FOR A BLACK GIRL

SOUL MEDICINE FOR A BLACK GIRL

Prayer:

God, why doesn't he love me?

Deeply explore this question with God. This may cause for you to go on an extended consecration and/or fast before the Lord. Trust his process.

"He" can be a father, a brother, a husband, or boyfriend. Whomever he is, this lack of love is breeding a spirit of rejection. This spirit is a hard spirit to break and will affect every relationship in a person's life if it goes unchecked.

What did you and God talk about? (write it here or in your journal)

_____

_____

_____

_____

_____

_____

_____

_____

_____

_____

_____

SOUL MEDICINE FOR A BLACK GIRL

SOUL MEDICINE FOR A BLACK GIRL

SOUL MEDICINE FOR A BLACK GIRL

Prayer:

God, why do I feel so trapped?

Deeply explore this question with God. This may cause for you to go on an extended consecration and/or fast before the Lord. Trust his process.

Some of us Black Girls function in the Black Church and feel purposeless. We feel trapped by religion but afraid to explore the world due to a fear of hell. Clearly, God doesn't intend for us to live like this. We must find our balance.

What did you and God talk about? (write it here or in your journal)

_____

_____

_____

_____

_____

_____

_____

_____

_____

_____

SOUL MEDICINE FOR A BLACK GIRL

SOUL MEDICINE FOR A BLACK GIRL

SOUL MEDICINE FOR A BLACK GIRL

Now that you had some provoking question presented to you, I'm sure you may have questions that you want to ask God that are more specific to your current life and season.

A conversation with God is nothing but prayer. But because we've been taught that it has to be done in one particular way, we get stuck and feel ineffective. There is no right or wrong way to talk to God, he just wants you to talk to him and acknowledge him.

The reason this book is not filled with scripture is because I want you to pick up your Bible yourself and explore. Be intentional about getting to know God and allow him to lead you. Because the scripture he may give me to help with the same question asked, may not be the scripture he wants to present to you.

We must know God for ourselves. The only way we get our own personal relationship is through the studying and personal reflection through his divine guidance.

-circapurple presents-

When a *Black Girl* Glows Up!

A 30-Day Conversation With Yourself

purchase of this book supports purple's flower film project

Glow up – (v.) the act of budding into the most phenomenal version of yourself.

WHEN A BLACK GIRL GLOWS UP

If you purchased this book as a whole or purchased the individual copy of *Soul Medicine for a Black Girl* then you'll know that I'm all about talking things out.

I think in the Black community we don't talk to ourselves enough. We don't talk to other people enough. We hold many things inside that become internalized and resurfaces into destruction.

But that's not what I'm here to talk about. I want to talk about glowing up and living our best lives. In order to live your best life, you must first know what you want out of life.

There's no deep introduction to the last book of this series, it's exactly what the cover said, "A 30-day Conversation with Yourself".

You can have this conversation with yourself in any way you want to. You can have an audible conversation as you go through the days. You can journal through the conversation. You can video record this conversation with yourself.

Whatever you do, make sure you have the conversation. The purpose is to acknowledge yourself. All aspects of you. To correct, build up, and refine who you are, and become a better version of yourself.

A deep, introspective look into your personal mirror. Only person there to judge you is yourself – working out yourself personally and privately.

Take it one day at a time and be very conscious about each day's question throughout your day.

CIRCAPURPLE PRESENTS

WHEN A BLACK GIRL GLOWS UP

This is a personal conversation, so the pronouns to be used is "I" and "my". And as you ask yourself the questions, say them out loud!

Well, let's get to it!

CIRCAPURPLE PRESENTS

WHEN A BLACK GIRL GLOWS UP

Day 1

What do I love?

CIRCAPURPLE PRESENTS

WHEN A BLACK GIRL GLOWS UP

Day 2

Why do I want what I want?

CIRCAPURPLE PRESENTS

WHEN A BLACK GIRL GLOWS UP

Day 3

What is my inner truth?

CIRCAPURPLE PRESENTS

WHEN A BLACK GIRL GLOWS UP

Day 4

What are my real goals?

CIRCAPURPLE PRESENTS

WHEN A BLACK GIRL GLOWS UP

Day 5

What am I willing to sacrifice for my goals?

CIRCAPURPLE PRESENTS

WHEN A BLACK GIRL GLOWS UP

Day 6

Have I celebrated any of my little victories lately?

CIRCAPURPLE PRESENTS

WHEN A BLACK GIRL GLOWS UP

Day 7

Have I helped anyone else lately? Why or Why not?

CIRCAPURPLE PRESENTS

WHEN A BLACK GIRL GLOWS UP

Day 8

Am I happy?

CIRCAPURPLE PRESENTS

WHEN A BLACK GIRL GLOWS UP

Day 9

What actually is my happiness?

CIRCAPURPLE PRESENTS

WHEN A BLACK GIRL GLOWS UP

Day 10

Who do I have unforgiveness toward?

CIRCAPURPLE PRESENTS

WHEN A BLACK GIRL GLOWS UP

Day 11

What is my inner dialogue?

CIRCAPURPLE PRESENTS

WHEN A BLACK GIRL GLOWS UP

Day 12

What plagues my spirit? How do I get rid of it?

CIRCAPURPLE PRESENTS

WHEN A BLACK GIRL GLOWS UP

Day 13

What do I need clarity about?

CIRCAPURPLE PRESENTS

WHEN A BLACK GIRL GLOWS UP

Day 14

What do other women teach me? Is it right? Is it wrong?

CIRCAPURPLE PRESENTS

WHEN A BLACK GIRL GLOWS UP

Day 15

What are my personal self-contradictions?

CIRCAPURPLE PRESENTS

WHEN A BLACK GIRL GLOWS UP

Day 16

What is the most painful thing I've been through thus far? Does it still have control over me?

CIRCAPURPLE PRESENTS

WHEN A BLACK GIRL GLOWS UP

Day 17

What am I proud of?

CIRCAPURPLE PRESENTS

WHEN A BLACK GIRL GLOWS UP

Day 18

What scares me?

CIRCAPURPLE PRESENTS

WHEN A BLACK GIRL GLOWS UP

Day 19

What do I need?

CIRCAPURPLE PRESENTS

WHEN A BLACK GIRL GLOWS UP

Day 20

What are my regrets? Should I pursue the things I gave up on?

CIRCAPURPLE PRESENTS

WHEN A BLACK GIRL GLOWS UP

Day 21

What accomplishment have I not rewarded myself for?

CIRCAPURPLE PRESENTS

WHEN A BLACK GIRL GLOWS UP

Day 22

Do I really know who am I and do others know it?

CIRCAPURPLE PRESENTS

WHEN A BLACK GIRL GLOWS UP

Day 23

Do I tell myself the truth?

CIRCAPURPLE PRESENTS

WHEN A BLACK GIRL GLOWS UP

Day 24

What do I use to mask my insecurities?

CIRCAPURPLE PRESENTS

WHEN A BLACK GIRL GLOWS UP

Day 25

What do I deserve?

CIRCAPURPLE PRESENTS

WHEN A BLACK GIRL GLOWS UP

Day 26

Am I doing what I must do or what I should do?

Read the book, *The Crossroads of Should and Must: Find and Follow Your Passion* by Elle Luna

CIRCAPURPLE PRESENTS

WHEN A BLACK GIRL GLOWS UP

Day 27

Do I challenge my own negative thoughts or let them influence me?

CIRCAPURPLE PRESENTS

WHEN A BLACK GIRL GLOWS UP

Day 28

When was the last time I was good to myself?

CIRCAPURPLE PRESENTS

WHEN A BLACK GIRL GLOWS UP

Day 29

Do I practice what I preach?

CIRCAPURPLE PRESENTS

WHEN A BLACK GIRL GLOWS UP

Day 30

Have I glowed up?

CIRCAPURPLE PRESENTS

About the Author

Ty Young is an author, blogger, graphic designer, and soon to be first time film maker.

She has written 3 prior works: *My Journey to Life* (pen-name Ty Waller), *The Uncertain Journey of Love & Marriage* (pen-name Ty Waller), and *Purple Potpourri & Sacred Vulnerability*.

In addition to releasing *The Black Girl Book Series*, she'll also be releasing *When Lust Has Conceived* (April 2019), *The Alpha Bid* (part of the Distinguished Gentlemen Anthology, May 2019), and *Rules of Engagement* (June 2019).

Check out her blog, CircaPurple, where she talks faith, soul and her opinion at circapurple.com.

Connect with her on Twitter @tywaller24; IG & Facebook @circapurple

www.ingramcontent.com/pod-product-compliance
Lightning Source LLC
Chambersburg PA
CBHW050635160426
43194CB00010B/1683